LACUS SOMNIORUM

I0005543

poems by

Douglas Delaney

Finishing Line Press
Georgetown, Kentucky

LACUS SOMNIORUM

ACKNOWLEDGMENTS

Tired Eyes—*Missouri Review*
Wet Dream and The Way You Are, The Way I'm Not—*Ploughshares*
Lingerie—*Harbinger*
Lacus Somniorum, Marble—*Butt Magazine*

Publisher: Leah Huete de Maines
Editor: Christen Kincaid
Cover Art: Teresa Delaney
Author Photo: Teresa Delaney
Cover Design: Elizabeth Maines McCleavy

Order online: www.finishinglinepress.com
also available on amazon.com

Author inquiries and mail orders:
Finishing Line Press
PO Box 1626
Georgetown, Kentucky 40324
USA

Contents

Wet Dream 1

Tired Eyes 2

Sea Lanes 3

Lingerie 4

The Way You Are, The Way I'm Not 5

Stop Horse Jade.. 6

Lost & Found 7

Return to You... 8

Lacus Somniorum 10

Raining... 11

Marble 12

Conversation 13

Shanghai Express.. 14

A Moment 15

Red Sweaters... 16

Autumn.. 17

Cheese 18

Portrait 19

Nile in the Morning 20

For Teresa
The witness & keeper of history

WET DREAM

Ocean currents spill dust
Underwater canyons extend
to African rivers
from the Congo and back
to the Orange Canyons
But it is not Atlantis
No, this is Walvis Ridge
Under the Atlantic
are deep troughs and long ridges
Moonless mountains to the Hawaiian Deep
and Johnson Island north to Musicians
Seamounts and the Mendocino Fracture
The Aleutian Trench borders
volcanic Kodiac Guyot that moves
east to the Great Trough
San Andreas Fault to Clipperton Ridge
then southeast to the Middle
America Trench or home—
the quiet corner of the great bowl
Pacific Ocean
Abysmal wonderland
of lights ending rain

TIRED EYES

At the far edge of visibility
is a point I'm heading toward,
to pass, then another point appears
still too distant to be visible.
A herd of animals will run for days
searching for water--
Who is breathing, moving
my legs one after the other?
Who is in my body, sleeping in my head?
Ducks sitting in the reservoir
occasionally dive, as trees
casually drift by.
An immovable object decides
to hurtle through space,
a flower is going back to seed.
In the furthest distance
clouds are mobilizing like an ocean.
An old memory is beginning to disappear
for someone reclined
on a horse, staring at the blades of grass
arranged in a field too large to cross.

SEA LANES

He was suffering in the cargo hold.
A retreat into a vale of contracts.
The dogs have gone home to their bones.

No one is sure if America will fit
into the museum. Japanese engineers
have designed the necessary machinery.
They could have built a house

without nails, or a language that seasons
nerve-endings with desire for change.
To build with what remains

is the largest job left. The plank,
and rope, spire and diphthong
hanging on Alice's ear. We will travel
light, perhaps by train and ship, we must

save the golden monuments that dot
history like blisters on the surface
of the moon. Lights go out. Neighborhoods

smoke their children. The shiny
vehicles seem almost angry with the gray
light of November. They give color
to this dull landscape.

The cargo hold is colder now.
Weather takes on an impertinence
we decide is left over by statues

no one remembers. The history of a language
is being charted in the street
by children running through leaves
shouting new names for objects they don't
recognize.

LINGERIE

It was a Chinese painting of bandaged
figures reaching into their future.
Or were they white ghosts leaving

through the grass roof of their house–
leaving the still heaving dragon to quiet
the barking dog and wailing baby.

At night notes were passed in baskets, delivered
by a third party and in a flurry of snow the lovers
met and the world continued without them.

Sometimes the fucking became so violent
the buildings shook and the animals
murmured in their sleep, walking and falling

off the world into seemingly cluttered nature.
Everyone knew better of course–the children scared
the adults into thinking this ending lasted forever

and the adults who knew better were friends
of the children while the animals posed
for nature photographs in the full moon over half the world.

THE WAY YOU ARE, THE WAY I'M NOT

The way the world is not the way you want the world
to be is not profound and does not surprise me.

The way you are the way you want to be in a world
you exist in regardless amazes me.

When you found out that the way I am in the world
is not the way I am and the way you looked

at me is the way I'll remember you looked.
And the next time I saw you, you let me know

it was okay to be the way I am, but I couldn't
because I thought I'd be more entertaining the way I'm not.

Then I didn't see you for a long time and became even
less the way I am until I did see you and you looked

and I remembered who you were. And it still amazed
me that you could be who you were in a world

which you didn't recognize as existing anyway.
The important thing you said was that if I recognized

the way the world is, is to be the way I am therefore
exist the way the world doesn't

And it's been good to know someone the way they really are
and for you to know me the way I can't.

STOP HORSE JADE
From "Bound Feet and Western Dress"

Your future is poised on a point
of green light. Long before the black
dreams of opium smoke
and lazy love. You sit on a couch
shadow carved anxiously
waiting for the right words.
Breaking with history and pressed
by tradition. How did you get here?
Are you building something or waiting
for a finer definition as you drift
through a cloudless meadow,
sheep and cow, grass blades gone awry.
Soon the question is answered
and your joy flung arms embrace
the welcoming air.

As the ring of green jade flies
like a piece of universe
to a settling way below the balcony
the message is clear and there
is no turning back. Today the horse
does not stop to graze but gallops
through the barriers of light
pounding the earth in joy and violence.

LOST & FOUND

Patience is a virtue only for those
who have no time left.

When these boulders emerge as prehistoric
birds and fly off you will understand.

On a journey to the other side of the planet
we became lost in the long night of Murmansk

The earth hardened and the frost-filled
grass stalks snapped under my feet; I was alone.

Old landscapes were recalled in a series of
snapshots, forgotten and remembered, and forgotten.

If you can't find a needle, get a baby,
the baby will find the needle.

Too much praise was a sign of failure,
No praise a recognition of loss; a ship

slipping from a lock, or your shadow
carrying you through warm winds to a strange place.

RETURN TO YOU

Raising your tired arms
you stare at the branches
of a willow trying to fly
off the surface of this planet
waving good-bye to you.
Good-bye. Without your
imagination we would be history.
Welcome home, this country
needs airing, this future needs
a future. Don't be confused
don't be displeased by our
expectations for you. They are grand.
You will fit in perfectly,
of course, so does everyone,
but you are special. The postcard
is thrown carelessly through
the mail slot, smoke enters
the same way as you spin it
into hoops you're careful not to jump
through. That old military training.

The rain continues to pound
vacationers into retreat but you
are glad to see them disappear
into steamy diners, why not?
In the sketchy landscape something
emerges. You can only love an idea
so long before you need identification
and this idea has been around for a long time.

Fields of girls hurl spears with resolute
joy and we applaud the effort.
We were born to love passion
in others. You walk out of the movie
with no idea of who you are
and that's the way it is for now.
The coastline smiles back at you.
The storm is changing direction,
and you are left untouched.
Returning home is a temporary
solution. You are left without a choice
but to return to where you are,
and who returns to you,
in the ceaseless reality of another
morning on the wrong continent
without a map without a compass.

LACUS SOMNIORUM
For June

In a single word a moan
filled your body then the room.

At this moment there no sense in running
for your life because you can't, everything is the same,

escape is impossible and you have always known
this though never believed it until now.

Somewhere they are tagging bodies at the hospital
morgue and sliding trays along in the cafeteria.

Outside a discussion is taking place,
as the wind lifts the undersides of leaves.

A few drops of rain hit an empty lake
and that is not the moon you recognize but your reflection.

You wish to walk around the lake, to pick up
stones and skip them across the surface, but this

is impossible. Not even a walk through a marbled
museum is possible now.

There is the long walk home
with the real moon to pass and notice,

and the cold snap of snow stinging your cheeks
as you look for warmth you can't find until you feel it.

Perhaps the first light you see will be your own
face noticing my empty gaze staring at you

As the final exaltations of life
play through your small body in such a hurry.

RAINING

Another day without control of the spirit world,
the city's auras are out of whack due to an electrical

storm so we stay in the cafes a little longer
than usual as rain pours off the awnings.

Huddled in doorways people stare at the sky
as if waiting for something different to happen.

Inside the smell of wet newspapers and coffee
is comforting, I remember days like this at camp.

When we couldn't be out torturing nature
or each other we stayed in and tortured various

compounds into shapes and designs. Mine would
be sloppy and poorly conceived, I didn't care

for the damp cement floor when I could be out
rattling through the rain. The city shakes

itself out and no one is in enough of a hurry
to leave a dry spot, it could go on like this all day.

MARBLE

There is so much lost in the tall weeds—
baseballs, one shoe, a stocking, even a necklace.
It is part of a continuous re-painting of a world.

You are fortunate to appear in a few of these scenes—
In the last one there was a terrific crash
of dishes, then symphonies of bird calls.

Later, more sounds of leaving—the purr of departure
in the sunset, like in the movies, red, blue, purple, and pink
emerged from the sky

and the stars arranged themselves
in their old places,
this is one way of looking at the world.

In another, I don't forget those sightless
moments when filtered splinters of air
lodged deep in our throats

to the inside of everything. To the vacant place
where your heart continues to pump
and the blood forgets to flow home.

CONVERSATION

I would tell you
but my lips are frozen
to your face
and we are locked in this embrace
that will last until
this conversation ends.

Afterwards
the obvious coastline
will review
the land and roll
over. And if
I wasn't so tired
I would remember
your name, our mission,

the music that
didn't play
and the clothes
you wore, your
quartz steps across the carpet
of forest without
a stick in the wrong place,

without any
idea of why we
are still here
licking each
other dry.

SHANGHAI EXPRESS

Anything is possible
if you know how to smoke
in the black and white
evening of the day before
everything took time to converge.
Converging to ensure
the moonlight illuminated
the tracks to your potential destination.
You are uncertain yet balanced
in the elegant smoke
of the dining car--a ruby
in an otherwise stark
necklace. The reunion
lasted only long enough
to be interrupted by chance.
Because of who you are
there is reason to believe
the ending is happening again.
You never change until you do.
The reflection of yourself
in the shop window is startling.
You are beckoned into the jewelers
only to learn that he was waving
to someone else. It is only
when you leave, cigarette poised
in your pouting lips that you
notice the flame at your mouth
is held by an arm not belonging to you.

A MOMENT

The desert sleeps along with the sleeper
taking shallow breathes, almost awake
beneath a quilt of stars shining through
the canopied sky.

The sleeper shifts, restless, sheetless
Until the dream gathers in the breeze
filled horizon. Time to go.

Back still wet
you drive on, the highway
is soft while headlights spray
butterfly shadows across a rainless
sky of invisible hands.

RED SWEATERS

Red sweaters are swell
when they are clinging
to your body like snow
on a mountain or orange
on the moon.

AUTUMN

You must believe in the mystical,
lawn chairs scatter the walkways,
useless ribs, meatless and shiny.
The horizon seems indifferent.
What can you do?
We have you where we want you--
needing air, trying to stay warm
in the shadows of fat apples,
hanging on branches, the harvest
heavy in the wet morning.

We have been trying to get this note
to you for a long time. The message
is brief, to the point. A hawk
lights on a swaying branch.
Spongy green ponds of grass
soften the landscape.
The hawk watches, seeing
only what moves. Move.

CHEESE

Laid out on a wood board thick
with scent, displayed in electric
yellow reflection. We are overwhelmed
by an eager eccentric. From mild
to sharp--Isle of Mull to Southern Ireland,
cheese that is soft and fragrant born
from Greta and Gretel staring at us
from bent black and white photo.
Unpasteurized and pure
for the tasting. The art of cheese is lost.
Eaten in clockwise rotation,
the order is crucial to this experience
but no more than the sweet port
and the film of love still fresh on our lips.

PORTRAIT

Cairo in July defies the heat
as do her long black gloves.
In the stillness of the mosque
she holds the camera
eyes focused on the screen.
What brings her to this spot
a long way from home
where her style meets history?
Arches float above the black and gold
walls where she blends
into hand-built nature, posing
as she gazes through the still
lens while answering an incoming call.

NILE IN MORNING

It's a long pull across.
Your green skiff moves with effort
low in water, heavy crates
of mango stacked in seeming chaos
but balanced perfectly.
Currents push you off course
and it's work keeping the bow straight.
I marvel at the effort and the red and green
striped oars painted with care
moving in the early sun.
Stopping mid-river, you glance
at the white crane staring back
at you. Resting at the stern.

Douglas grew up in the wilds of New Jersey. He eventually settled in the Boston area after a stint in New Hampshire for high school. He wrestled with the thought of being either a logger or an actor before deciding on letting the universe determine his future. The universe decided he should teach in the Emerson College Creative Program. Later, he worked as a management consultant specializing in innovation and strategic marketing for Fortune 500 companies. He is also well known for a remarkable list of celebrity sightings, interactions and potential friendships.

Today he has relocated to Hoboken, NJ, where he enjoys a slight view of the Empire State Building from his living room. He lives with his wife Teresa and their young Shiba Inu, Pretzel who **is** both demanding and mysterious.